Why has this booklet been

This booklet was originally written for the UK nuclear new build organisations as a general introduction to the IT systems that will support the safe and effective management of the completed power station during its commissioning, operational and decommissioning phases. It's principles can be used by other industries to compare how they implement similar systems

The asset management system's prime purpose is as an essential aid to ensure the plant is operated and maintained within the assumptions / parameters of the safety case and other statutory obligations

The booklet describes the importance of collecting information and data throughout the life of the new nuclear build process constructing the digital twin (Virtual Plant) alongside the physical plant. The data will be transitioned into the operational power station systems. It emphasises that it is crucial that the information collected during the life of the new build Project phase is complete, true, findable and, when it is found, can be trusted.

In describing the EAM, the booklet inevitably also describes how the nuclear site will operate. Its processes and the information it will need to support these processes.

This document, by its nature, can only be a very superficial overview of the role of an EAM solution in the management of an operational nuclear station and if anyone wants further detail then they should contact the author.

For further information, you may also wish to read the related booklets:

CONFIGURATION MANAGEMENT
FOR BEGINNERS

BUILDING THE VIRTUAL
NUCLEAR POWER PLANT

Enterprise Asset Management for Beginners

WE'RE BUILDING MORE THAN A NUCLEAR POWER STATION

Words written and pictures drawn by Martin Wakeman

What's in this book?

What's in this booklet?

Why do we need an EAM?

A nuclear power station can be thought of as a single large machine with some very complicated parts.

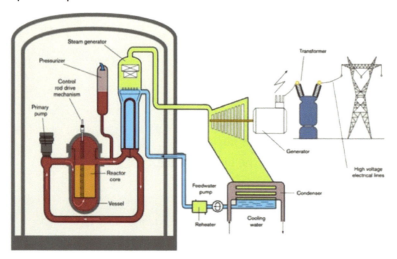

Whilst this machine is running to its optimum, the company is generating income (cash). When the machine is not running the company is losing money.

So the aim of any operating power station is to safely keep the machine running continuously for as long as possible.

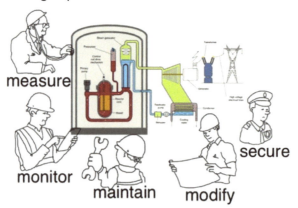

The nuclear station machine is designed to operate for a long time. It is designed with redundancy so that certain elements of the machine can be taken off line at any one time and the machine still functions safely.

What is an EAM?

An Enterprise Asset Management (EAM) system is a very large Information Management system that covers a wide variety of functional areas that would traditionally be catered for by many separate IT systems

This booklet will attempt to describe each of these functional areas and how each will contribute to the well-being and management of the operational station.

WHY IS IT CALLED AN EAM?

IS THE EAM ONE SYSTEM?

The Digital Twin or Virtual Power Plant

The new nuclear power station has been designed to operate safely and efficiently!

But to operate the station will also need a skilled workforce, detailed processes **and accurate and accessible information** (in documents, drawings, 3D models, data and records managed in IT systems) to enable lifetime, safe, effective and efficient operation of the station

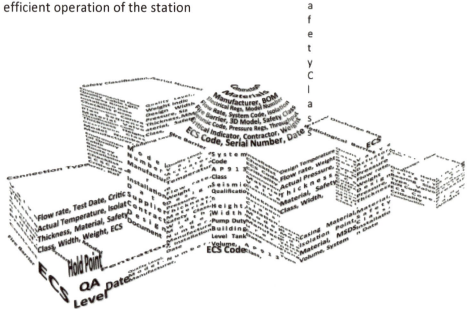

The Virtual Power Plant initiative will help the station operations by collecting and validating all the information (documents, drawings, models and Asset Information) so that it can be found and trusted by operations years into the future

The EAM and Virtual Power Plant will help pay for the new build station

The nuclear new build project is accumulating £billions in debt that must be paid off before the power station starts to accumulate profit for the owners.

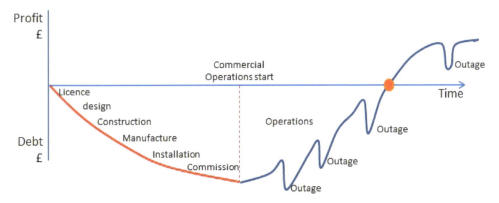

The rate at which the new plant becomes profitable will be dependent on the safe, effective and efficient operation of the station. As mentioned above, the key to this is minimising the number and the length of outages when the station is not generating.

For instance, Hinkley Point C will have a planned outage every 18 months. The length of each outage will depend on the type of Outage:
  ROO Refuelling Only Outage (15 days)
  NRO Normal Refuelling Outage (26 days)
  ISIO In-Service Inspection Outage (60 days)
To keep to (or improve on) these business case durations will depend upon, to some extent, the effective use of the EAM solution and the immediate availability of a trusted and complete set of data for all affected assets.

How can the EAM help with keeping the plant running?

The EAM system will be one of the most important "**Information**" systems of the operating plant (Two other major "information systems" are the Process and Safety Instrumentation and Control (I&C) system and the collection of information that constitutes the Station's Operational Safety Case. (The safety case is realised mainly through documents but parts will be managed by the TechSpec compliance aspects of the EAM – see later)

The Enterprise Asset management system is multi-facetted system. It is one large IT system performing many different roles.
Each person using the EAM will see and act upon different elements of the same data.

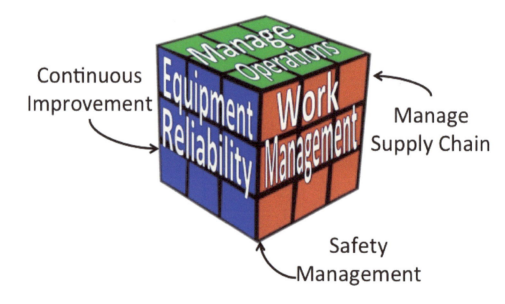

This booklet will guide the reader through how each suite of functional components work and interact but at the core of the EAM is the central data core and its management.

The EAM has a common core data set

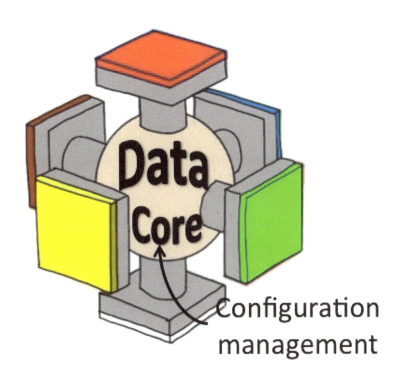

Configuration management

The Operational phase of HPC will need a comprehensive and correct set of data and it is the goal of the Virtual Plant initiative within the HPC project to build and validate that data and make sure it is available to Operations when they need it.

What is in this Core Data Set?
It is the set of data that will be handed over to operations from the project and, as part of the Data Centric Virtual Plant initiative; this will be a far more comprehensive set of data than has ever been gathered in a nuclear new build before to ensure the best possible safe, effective and efficient operation of the plant.

What is in the core data set? -1

Data will include

Asset Information. (Assets also known as **Systems, Structures and Components** in the nuclear industry or the **Master Equipment List** or the **Master Tag Register** in other industries). In operations terms, it is the list of all maintainable identified items on the power station.

Every system, structure and component on the plant is tagged or labelled with the **Functional Identification Code**. In EDF, they call it the ECS Code, In other sites, its called the KKS or RDS-PP code. It is a label created by the designers that is then used throughout the full lifecycle of the plant. Design, build, operate, decommission.

Every item (Systems, Structures and Components (SSC)) on the plant will be labelled with the code)

A civil **structure** is something that is built rather than manufactured. For example: a building, a room, Steelwork, a gallery, a staircase.

A **component** is something that is manufactured or purchased such as pumps,

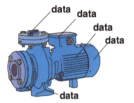

valves, motors. The distinction between structures and components doesn't really matter in an EAM sense; both are maintainable or could have a safety function or need to be inspected. Some items such as doors or pipework could be thought of as either a structure or a component.

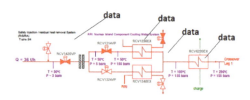

A **system** is a collection of interrelated components (and structures) which perform a function on the power station. Such as the Emergency Lighting system or the Diesel Building Ventilation System.

What is in the core data set? -2

Bills of Material (BOM)

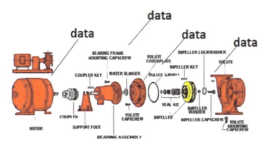

data
data
data
data

A Bill of Materials is a collection of sub-components that make up a component. And is most likely supplied by the manufacturer of the equipment item. The reason why the BOM is important is that the station may decide to stock some of the items on the BOM in order to perform maintenance on the Component.

Other items such as special tools and consumables (oil, gloves, gaskets) may also be needed to maintain the component.

One important type of information for operations to gather will be the Material Items which will be used in the maintenance and testing of every component on the site. Some of these Material Items will be kept in the site stores whilst some will be purchased on an as-needed basis.

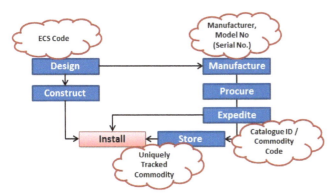

Data can be "attached" at different stages of the build process and different identifiers are used by different processes. The design is built around ECS codes; a manufacturer will produce a model no. to fulfil that design. It may be procured or stored using catalogue IDs and may be tracked during its lifetime by a UTC number. It is the installation process that brings all these islands of data together onto the plant.

Documents and Records Management

Firstly, lets identify the difference between "Documents" and "Records" from an operational station point of view. The HPC project will produce many millions of documents (including drawings) during the design and build phase. These will be

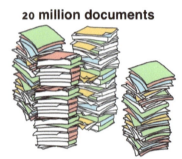

20 million documents

handed over to the operational phase of the station's lifetime but Operations will only commit to manage a small sub-set of these documents in a configured state. i.e. It will take a small subset of these documents and keep them up to date as operations continue. The others it will classify as "Records". The information in a Record is a statement at a particular time. The as-built set of documents and drawings are one such set of documents that will be kept up to date for the lifetime of the station.

In addition to the documents it gets from the HPC project, The pre-Operations team will have to build a suite of documents to manage the station: Plant Operating Instructions, Maintenance Instructions, Management Systems manuals, Technical Specifications (see later) etc.

The EAM system will be expected to "manage" Documents and Records for the operational site. It may do this in conjunction with another system.

Document management

Is managing the configured set of controlled documentation within the Company so that it is prepared, reviewed and approved by assigned personnel, to ensure that the documentation is legible, readily identifiable and available at the point of use.

Records Management

Is managing the requirements associated with identifying, collecting, indexing, filing, storing, maintaining and disposing of records.

Configuration Management

Managing changes to the configuration – The Engineering Change Process.

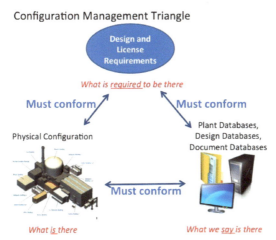

Configuration Management Triangle

The configuration management principle that in an **operational plant**, the configuration data held electronically in the plant databases **must conform** to the physical configuration of the plant and **must conform** to the design and licence requirements.

- **The purpose of the new build project is to build this triangle.**
- **The purpose of plant Operations is to maintain it.**
- **The maintenance of the configuration management triangle will be done through the Operations Engineering Change process controlled (in some part) by the EAM.**

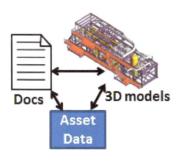

The virtual plant initiative will produce a wealth of 3D model and Asset information which will revolutionise the way that engineering change will be performed when compared to existing nuclear plants but the fundamentals of changing plant (and documents and processes) in a controlled and safe way will remain the same.

Engineering Change

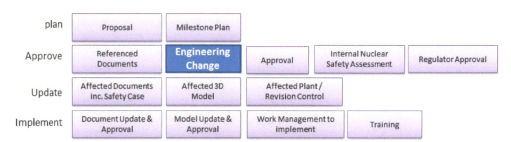

Any proposed change to the configuration management equilibrium. For instance modifications to Safety Cases, Processes and Plant installed and commissioned within the licensed site boundary must go through the **Engineering Change process**.

As must any proposed experiments and non-routine tests, which change the state of the plant in a manner which may affect nuclear safety

The EAM system, (in conjunction with others maybe?) will manage:

> Changes to documents, and other data including the 3D model
> Changes to the physical plant.
> Managing the safety case
> Planning of the change and any submissions to the internal and external regulator

It must ensure the design integrity of the plant.

Graded Approach of Quality Assurance

> Plant systems on a Nuclear Power Station differ in their significance, hence controls applied to activities undertaken or items procured must be proportional to their significance. Differentiation is achieved by a graded approach to Quality Assurance (QA) derived from a risk assessment based upon risk to nuclear safety, people's health and safety, breach of site licence, environment or statutory requirements, cost penalty, or loss of generation.

Manage Supply Chain

As with the rest of the EAM solution, the supply chain is geared towards ensuring the power station is kept running and so must be aligned with the maintenance plans: both the work week management plan and the outage plan (see later). Each material item will have its own strategy. Will it be kept in the site store, the supplier's store, purchased as required? It will depend on the criticality of the plant it services, the lead time, the cost, the risk and the maintenance strategy. Keeping items in stores just-in-case they are required has a cost associated with it and this needs to be balanced with the risk of not having the item available.

All the normal elements of a supply chain must be supported by the EAM but with some nuclear-specific nuances.

Purchasing & Contract management

The EAM will manage (possibly alongside other systems) the standard Purchasing and Contract management processes for obtaining goods and services: Preparation of specifications, assessment of bids, selection of suppliers, management of the resultant contracts, the purchase of goods and services providing a consistent approach to materials management

Manage Supply Chain - cont

Spares and materials may be graded depending upon the nuclear and industrial safety significance and potential financial loss that could occur due to failure. This determines the level of inspection, certification, documentation and control required during manufacture, procurement, repair and storage.

Inventory management

Material is procured to appropriate standards and procedures by suitably trained and experienced staff who ensure material is correctly procured, received, inspected, stored and issued. Stocking levels are reviewed to maximise inventory efficiency.

An appropriate **Materials Management Strategy** is developed for each item: Stocked or Non-Stocked, Critical Spares, Call-Off Orders, Vendor Managed Inventory, Consignment Stock strategies are all employed

Inventory Planning

Stock models and skilled practitioners examine – Lead Times, Safety stocks, Rarely Used Stocks, Economic Order Quantities, Outage and Planned Maintenance schedules and likelihood of emergent work based on equipment reliability data

Tools Management

Specialist tools including Measurement and Test Equipment (M&TE) alongside their calibration will be managed

Procurement Engineering / Equivalent parts

Only "compliant" plant spares are procured, stocked, repaired and installed in the Power Station.

It is a Nuclear Site Licence condition that the site maintains control of any modifications to plant which could occur through the substitution of spares and materials that are not in accordance with original design for use on plant.

MSDS / COSHH

The MSDS process covers the requirements for storage, use, special handling, and disposal for chemicals.

The MSDS module is the Master Chemical Data Repository. Its integrity and accuracy is paramount in maintaining an effective and quality tool.

Continuous Improvement – Organisational Learning (Learning by Experience)

Alongside document management, this should be the process most well-known to members of a new build project as an Organisational Learning programme should be one of the earliest processes established.

In an operational station the process, (which also encompasses Corrective Action Programme (CAP), Condition Reports (CR) Operational Experience (OPEX)), Action Tracking is closely linked to the management of the site and therefore the EAM solution

Condition Reports are raised based on internal or external operating experience in order to learn from others and is reported in a timely manner to reduce the potential for recurring /repeat events at the locations, and as appropriate, across the industry.

Each condition is appropriately screened to select, classify and prioritise events requiring further evaluation/investigation, according to their consequences, frequency and relevance to other locations. In addition, suitable analysis is performed on appropriate events, depending on their severity or frequency, to ensure that identified root causes and corrective actions are acted upon in a timely manner.

Continuous Improvement – Equipment Reliability

The Equipment Reliability programme will be based around the industry best practice described in the standard Institute of Nuclear Power Operations (INPO) document AP-913.

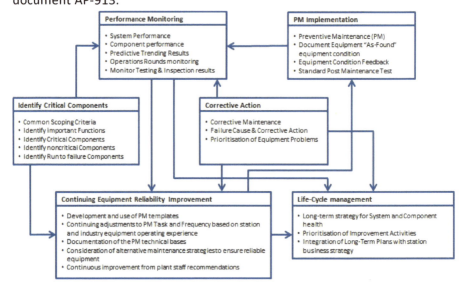

The objective is to ensure Equipment performs reliably between statutory/refuelling outages, and standby safety equipment operates properly upon demand. To ensure
Equipment is capable of satisfactory performance under all design conditions

This process includes activities normally associated with such programs as reliability centred maintenance, preventive maintenance (periodic and predictive), life cycle management and equipment performance monitoring.

The equipment reliability process represents the integration and coordination of a broad range of equipment reliability activities into one process for plant personnel to evaluate important station equipment, develop and implement a long-term maintenance plan, monitor equipment performance, and make continuing adjustments to preventive maintenance tasks and frequencies based on equipment operating experience.

Continuous Improvement – Elements of an Equipment Reliability Strategy

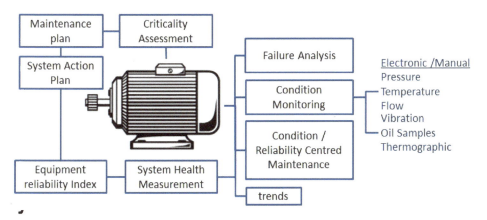

Identifying critical components

Critical equipment is identified based on importance to safety function, safe shutdown capability and power generation capability.

Performance Monitoring / Condition Monitoring

Equipment and system performance criteria established, performance monitored, adverse trends identified and corrective actions implemented and verified for effectiveness.

Failure Analysis

Failures and failure causes of concern are identified for critical equipment and measures are established to prevent them.

Measuring systems Health, Component Health (Asset Health)

Predictive maintenance technologies are implemented for critical equipment to detect equipment degradation and optimise equipment performance.

Equipment reliability Index /Systems Health Indicator Program

The System Health Indication Programme (SHIP) is a composite indicator used to gauge the overall performance of plant systems and components. It uses a combination of an overall score, colour-coding and detailed scores for the supporting metrics to allow the development of targeted **System Action Plans** *to continually drive improvements in Equipment reliability.*

Continuous Improvement – Asset Investment

The station will operate for a long time. Over its lifetime, the plant will need investment in order to maintain or improve its capability. Investment in nuclear power stations is usually very costly and investment decisions must be driven by data determining where to invest and when.

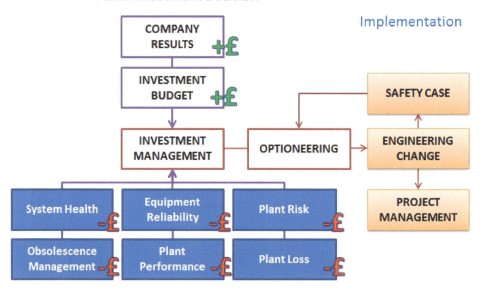

The EAM will provide much of the information required to make that investment and will manage its implementation through the Engineering Change process.

Managing Operations – What EAM does not do!

The Operations control room is where two major **Information Management** systems come together. The EAM does not include the Instrumentation and Control (I&C) architecture which comprises all the automation and safety systems for safe operations by allowing continuous monitoring and control of the plant parameters

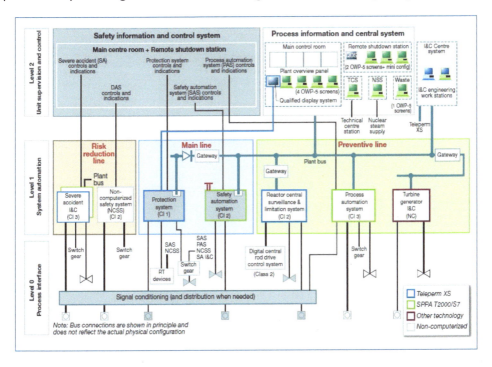

Nevertheless, there is a relationship in that the I&C measurements and control

signals come from plant components that are maintained through the EAM system. Much of that Interface is through a "Human" Interface in the control room where Operators bring together the two information worlds.

The Tech Spec process also brings these two Information worlds together.

Managing Operations – Tech Specs

UK Nuclear Site Licence Condition 23, (Operating Rules) ensures that a safety case is produced to demonstrate the safety of operations, that all the conditions and limits necessary in the interest of safety are identified, and that operations are, at all times, conducted in accordance with those limits  and conditions. In HPC these limits and conditions will be contained within the "Technical Specifications" and associated documentation. LC23 supports compliance with Licence Condition 27 (Safety mechanisms, devices and circuits). The conditions and limits necessary for safety of operations are contained in Technical Specifications.

Environmental conditions for operation of environmentally significant plant are contained in Environmental Specifications.

HANG ON: WHAT ARE TECHNICAL SPECIFICATIONS?

"Tech Specs" and "Limiting Conditions of Operation"

The term "Technical Specifications (or Tech Specs) means different things in different industries. In the nuclear Industry, the term "Tech Spec" represents a suite of documents and data that describes how the station must be operated to ensure safety.

Simply put, HPC will be safe because

it is designed to be safe,

it is constructed to be safe and

it is operated and maintained to be safe.

The Tech Specs will reference the critical elements of plant and describe the limits in which each element must operate. Plant information from instruments, tools and observations must be regularly checked (work scheduled by the EAM) to monitor compliance with the Tech Spec.

The Tech Specs are very prescriptive and will dictate what must happen if there is any deviation from the limiting conditions of operation and may ultimately lead to the shutdown of the station.

Managing Operations – Operator Observations

Plant Walkdowns

A Plant Walkdown is the mechanism used for performing a field evaluation of system performance and condition. The walkdown forms an essential part of system performance monitoring and the feedback from such walkdowns can be used to provide information for System Health reports and provide input to the Work  Management process. It is also a key requirement of the System Health Assessment Process.

Plant walkdowns complement the routine inspections and surveillances performed by Operations staff and informal inspections by System Health Engineers (SHEs). The main objective is to review the physical condition and provide an assessment of the functionality of plant equipment.

Operators log

This is both a narrative and a structured record of **everything** that happens during the shift. It forms the basis of the handover from one shift to another and a permanent record of events on the station.

The Operators Logs form part of compliance with Licence Condition 25 – Operational Records.

Work Management

Work Management

All work on the operational power station should be performed using a common work management process controlled by the EAM. The Work management process therefore applies to the scheduling and execution of all preventative maintenance (PM) and non-preventative maintenance programme activities, surveillance tests and any related support activities. The scope of process and supporting processes include:

1. Identification and Prioritisation of Work

2. Long Term Planning (Cycle Plan)

3. Preparation, Execution and Performance Review of Work (Execution Plan)

4. PM Delivery Programme

The **Work Management** processes implemented at the operational plant will be based on Best Practice identified within the INPO AP-928 document and other standards such as ISO 55000 (I am working with the IAEA to produce guidance on this topic)

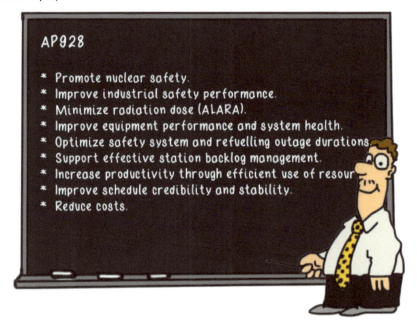

AP928

* Promote nuclear safety.
* Improve industrial safety performance.
* Minimize radiation dose (ALARA).
* Improve equipment performance and system health.
* Optimize safety system and refuelling outage durations.
* Support effective station backlog management.
* Increase productivity through efficient use of resour
* Improve schedule credibility and stability.
* Reduce costs.

Work Management – What Work needs to be done

What Work needs to be done?

Work management can generally be categorised into a few generic types:

Maintenance work where there is a physical interaction with an item of plant (such as a service or repair). The **routine** gathering of observations and measurements through which the equipment health is monitored. The more intelligence we can bring to these measurements, the more we can reduce potentially costly and risky physical maintenance.

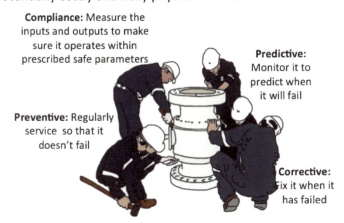

Compliance: Measure the inputs and outputs to make sure it operates within prescribed safe parameters

Predictive: Monitor it to predict when it will fail

Preventive: Regularly service so that it doesn't fail

Corrective: Fix it when it has failed

Statutory work Some jobs such as Scaffold, fire detectors, lifting equipment, pressure vessel inspections, environmental monitoring are statutory requirements that must be done on a given frequency (e.g. yearly, six monthly)

Maintenance Strategy

The development of a comprehensive maintenance strategy for every system, structure and component (SSC) is a key job for the operations team remembering that there may be 500,000 SSC's to consider.

The objective of the maintenance strategy is to ensure that the effective preventive maintenance tasks are performed on the correct equipment at the appropriate time, in order to achieve high reliability and availability of the plant. The core elements of this strategy are the identification of critical components, to record those items that have a significant impact on safety, reliability and generation, and the preventive maintenance (PM) review to determine applicable and effective maintenance tasks.

Work Management – How will work be performed?

How will the Work be performed? The answer is "safely"

Like everything else in the nuclear industry, all work must be performed in a very prescriptive and safe way. The work Order card (whether electronic or paper) will detail the steps to be taken, the tools (including Maintenance and test equipment) and parts required, the skills and qualifications required to perform the work. A series of other documents will be attached: A Risk assessment will assess all the potential hazards, A safety document will detail how those hazards are addressed and the precautions to be taken. Whilst some work will require Radiological or other Work Permits or selected person reports such as from a Chemist. A pre-Job brief will be performed and the area of work isolated if applicable..
The EAM must be hard-wired to ensure that safety is the overriding priority.

When should work be done?

Some minor corrective maintenance can be performed immediately

Through a process sometimes called a "Fix it Now" or "Diagnose and Rectification Team" (DART) or "Toolpouch" process. But most corrective work, especially when on safety related or critical equipment items will need to be planned alongside work generated by the Preventive Maintenance (PM) schedule. The planned execution of work will usually start many weeks out from when the work is executed in a System-Aligned Work-Week (SAWW) planning process.

Work Management – When should work be done? System Aligned Work Windows

The principle behind System Aligned Work Windows (SAWW) is to examine the risks of equipment being taken out of service (for maintenance) and the consequent impact that the loss of that plant will have on operational safety. By considering the functions lost, the SAWW process can offer time slots that minimise the operational risk. For example, if two pumps provide lubrication to a turbine bearing then both pumps should not be removed from service at the same time when the turbine is in operation.

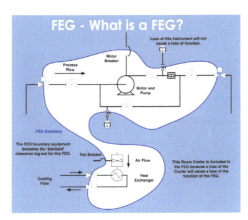

Safety related plant is categorised into functional equipment groups (FEG) which will segregate a collection of related equipment items of equipment which should be maintained as a whole. The simplest grouping will be the equipment item itself and the related equipment that will enable the isolation of the plant

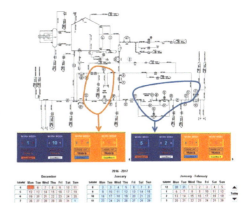

Each functional equipment group will then be nominated a work window in a 12 or 15-week rolling schedule so that any corrective or scheduled maintenance of that plant area will be planned at least 12 or 15 weeks ahead. Each Work Week is allocated a planner whose role is to ensure the safe and effective execution of the work within that week including materials and resource planning and ensuring all work is authorised and safety permits are in place

Work Management – Emergency work and Outage Planning

Emergency Work

Obviously in the System Aligned Work Week process, emergency situations may arise when the work cannot wait. In this case the existing work in the week will be examined and possibly delayed to ensure the safe operation of the plant.

Outage Planning

There are two scheduling methods in use at a power station. The Work Week Window process and the Outage Management Process

There are two types of outage: Unplanned (forced) and Planned. Unplanned shutdowns along with outage extensions and load reductions during power operations will hit the stations ability to hit its targets as calculated in its business case and the EAM and the documents and data built in the virtual plant initiative will contribute to preventing these issues and managing the plant back to service.

ISIO – NRO – ROO – NRO – ROO – NRO

*18 months
between outages*

There are three types of Planned Outage: **ISIO**= In-Service Inspection Outage (60 days)
NRO= Normal Refuelling Outage (26 days)
ROO= Refuelling Only Outage. **(15 days).**

NO work should be planned during the refuelling Only Outage which means that Outage work can only be performed every 36 months.

The EAM must be strongly coupled to a powerful planning tool like Primavera for both Work Week and Outage planning

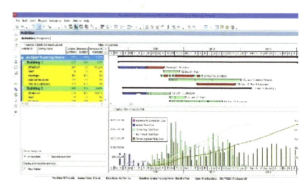

Safety Management & Total Exposure

The Safety Management process managed within the EAM must ensure that work is performed to the appropriate safety rules (E&M). These rules indicate the safety documents (permits for work) applicable, operational testing and the management of plant isolation activities, locks and keys.

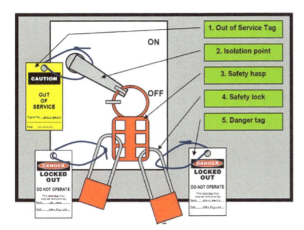

Isolation process includes. **Risk Assessment for the isolation work, Consent** to release the plant from the Control Room (if required), Carry out the Isolation Checklist steps to isolate the plant and confirm **Allocate the keys** to Key Safes and complete the entire Isolation Checklist.

Completion of any cross locking if required, allocate the Key Safe and lock it.

Risk Assessment

The Risk Assessment performed for each task must identify all hazards and the control measures to be adopted. Specialists including chemists, health physicists, industrial safety engineers, occupational health advisors, Senior Authorised Persons (SAPs) and nuclear safety group staff will assess each task as appropriate and recommend the safety documentation and activities that must be followed

Total Exposure Management

Additional radiological protection methods may also be managed within the EAM including the management of

Respiratory Protective Equipment (RPE)
Radiological Work Permit (RWP)
Radiological Surveys
Radiological Instruments
Radioactive sources
Health Physicists Daily Log (Radcon)

Manage People and Qualifications

Qualifications

In order to ensure safe and effective working, the applicable skills and qualifications required for each task must be specified in the work instruction and the EAM needs to ensure that tasks are performed by qualified individuals.

For example, maintenance personnel may be required to have a special security clearance before entering a building where work is to be done. A crane operator must have an in-date qualification for the specific type of crane.

By linking qualifications to work, planners and schedulers are able to assign appropriate personnel to jobs knowing that these individuals are qualified to perform the work properly.

An individual's qualification status must be kept up to date. Many qualifications are time-based and may be liable to expiry and refreshment

Labour Availability and Usage

Managing the total cost of work against each plant item: materials, people, contract spend is a key contributor to the investment management process on repair/replace decisions and in the investment management and risk management processes and improving efficiency as part of continuous improvement. Collecting labour time should be as automated as possible and should not lead to an administrative burden.

Labour availability, absence management will assist the work schedulers to ensure an efficient management of skills and qualifications

Why is it called an EAM? Is the EAM one system?

EAM = Enterprise Asset Management is just a name conjured by vendors and consultants to sell software and vendors. Other confusingly similar terms include ERP= Enterprise Resource Planning, ECM= Enterprise Content Management, ALM= Asset Lifecycle Management, PLM=Product/Project Lifecycle Management are similar terms which group together related functionality. What adds confusion is that many of these systems suites contain overlapping functionality and each vendor type is trying to move into the other's territory. We can and we will call this thing something other than EAM. For one thing, we don't call ourselves an "Enterprise"

Is the EAM one system? – Probably not. One system cannot fulfil all the requirements in this booklet so systems will have to be integrated. In EDF Energy NG then their Asset Suite system covers a lot of this functionality but their system has direct interfaces to other systems and other systems extract and use the data from the core system

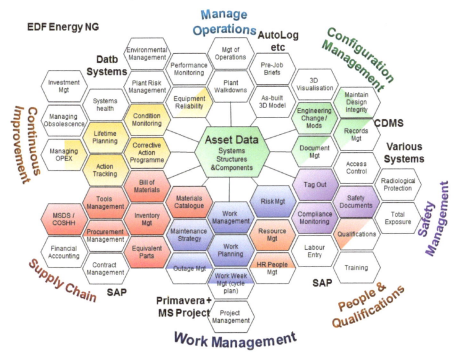

Building the EAM in a nuclear new build environment

Building the EAM

The EAM capability will be built during the HPC power plant build process. Assets (Systems Structures and Components) will be built alongside the related documents drawings and records associated with each Asset. But alongside that will be a comprehensive set of as-built 3D model data describing the configuration of the plant plus potentially 4D (time) and 5D (cost) sequences which will revolutionise how engineering design change will be performed in the future.

In fact, a better name for EAM should be ALM: **"Asset Lifecycle Management"** and many software vendors now market themselves in this way

Definitions

ALARP As Low As Reasonably Practicable

Applicable The characteristic of a PM task when it is capable of improving the reliability of the component by decreasing its failure rate.

Availability The fraction of time that a component is able to perform its intended function when it is required to be available for service.

BAT Best Available Techniques

Bill of Materials (BOM) A BOM is a list of materials/spares (catalogue items) required to maintain an Equipment item

BPM Best Practicable Means, a demonstration that the selected option is the most practicable way of achieving the required objective

Catalogue spares. Spares recorded within EAM materials catalogue

Commercial Grade Dedication Process used to provide assurance that items not specifically produced for nuclear applications will perform as required to support their safety function.

Component A piece of equipment, such as a pump, valve, motor or instrument.

Component Failure Loss of ability of a component to perform one or more of its intended functions.

Condition Monitoring. Tests and inspections that can be accomplished on an unobtrusive basis to identify a potential failure. Condition monitoring includes established predictive maintenance techniques.

Configuration control Making sure that all documents and drawings are aligned with actual plant status and operating parameters

Controlled Document Documents that are subject to revision must be approved, auditable and their distribution controlled to ensure current copy usage.

Corrective Maintenance. Repair and restoration of component or components that have failed or are malfunctioning and are not performing their intended function..

COSHH Control of substances hazardous to health

Critical Equipment or Critical Component Critical Equipment or Components are items that, if they fail, cause significant effect to plant for example: by causing a Reactor Trip, or significant load reduction, or an unplanned limited Condition of Operation.

Cycle Plan A plan maintained by the organisation for a determined number of cycles into the future. The plan is detailed to work order level and is managed for proper operational risk alignment of the work and rough resource alignment to

Definitions

Defect and Rectification Team (DART) A self-contained team capable of responding to priority work required to be done and not placed in the scheduling process **Defect Tag** A visual indication that a defect has been identified.

Defect Work This type of work, is raised by personnel on site using the defect tagging system and electronic work request, when plant/equipment is not meeting its design requirements

ECS Code EDF Coding System is a structured functional code developed by the designers and used throughout the lifetime of the plant describing every system, structure and component on the station

Emergent Work Any work that is added to the station master work schedule after schedule freeze.

EPRI Electric Power Research Institute

ERI Equipment Reliability Index

Failure Cause The physical mechanisms or reasons that produced the failure.

Failure Rate The actual or expected number of failures for a given type of component in a given time period. For example, the failure rate of a capacitor can be specified as the number of short circuit failures per million capacitor-hours. While the failure rate of an item is often a function of time, it also may depend on such factors as the number of operating cycles or environmental conditions.

Fragnets A number of related detailed activities within, or across work week schedules that are grouped together through the use of a specific scheduling code. This grouping enables the correct focus on preparation and execution of the overall specific task or project

Function The actions or requirements that a component or system must accomplish, sometimes defined in terms of performance capabilities.

Functional Equipment Group (FEG) A functional equipment group identifies all the systems, structures or components through a designation (FEG number) which are functionally related to a particular piece of Primary Equipment (PE). Because of this relationship whenever the piece of primary equipment is isolated the equipment in the FEG also becomes available to perform work on.

Permanent Record A record (also referred to as a Lifetime Record) to be held for the lifetime of the plant, item or activity including decommissioning or any other legally specified period, whichever is the longer.

Plant Modification (AKA Engineering Change) A change to existing plant, new plant, processes, safety cases or defeat of interlocks

Definitions

Functional Failure A failure of a function that results in a loss of system function(s). The failure may be active or passive, evident or hidden.

Hazard The potential to cause harm, including ill health and injury; damage to property, plant products or the environment; production losses or increased liabilities.

IAEA International Atomic Energy Agency

INPO Institute of Nuclear Power Operations

Life-Cycle Management The integration of ageing management and economic planning to optimise the operation, maintenance and service life of SSC, maintain an acceptable level of performance and safety and maximise return of investment over the service life of the plant.

Low Significance A maintenance strategy to allow selected components to operate until functional failure without performing preventive maintenance on the components (also known as Run to Failure).

Maintenance Strategy The approach used to ensure that effective preventive tasks are carried out on the correct equipment.

Measuring and Test Equipment (M&TE) Equipment used to test, calibrate, measure, or fault find on other items of equipment and is calibrated at specified intervals against National Standards. M&TE is used to make measurements when accuracy and quality of results is needed to meet Statutory and Mandatory requirements.

Model Work Order A MWO is created by the Specifier and is a Work Order template to enable generation of 'live work' from a PMRQ

Predefined Maintenance Requirement (PMRQ) The PMRQ is an identified need to carry out a predefined maintenance activity for compliance, statutory or preventative maintenance requirements and is identified by the system owner

MSDS Material safety data sheet

Obsolete Where equipment is no longer available due to cessation of manufacturing, service or support, and exhaustion of spares

Obsolescence Where equipment is to become obsolete, where a manufacturer decides to longer manufacture a product or provide a service or support

OEM Original Equipment Manufacturer

OPEX Operating Experience – not to be confused with **OPEX** = Operational Expenditure

Planned Maintenance is a form of preventive maintenance consisting of refurbishment or replacement that is scheduled and performed to preclude failure

Definitions

Predictive Maintenance A form of preventive maintenance performed continuously or at intervals governed by observed condition to monitor, diagnose or trend SSC functional or condition indicators. Results indicate current and future functional ability or the nature of and schedule for planned maintenance.

Preventative Maintenance (PM) Includes predictive (condition-based) and periodic/planned (timebased) actions taken to maintain a piece of equipment within design operating conditions and to extend its life.

PM Categories a sub categorisation of types of Preventive Maintenance for management and reporting purposes: Includes: Condition Monitoring, Licensing, Mandatory, Maintenance Schedule, Technical Specification, Statutory, Environmental Maintenance Schedule, Fire Systems, Routine Critical, Routine Activity, Routine Event

Primary Equipment Groups A group of primary pieces of equipment that are arranged within the site's System Aligned Work Windows to be isolated together in a designated work week ensuring operational safety and generation while providing proper windows for performing intrusive and non-intrusive work

Post Maintenance Test

This work order task is raised by the work order specifier to ensure that plant/equipment meets its design requirements on completion of the maintenance process.

Qualification: The combination of an individual's attributes and technical, academic, and supervisory knowledge and skills development via training, education, and demonstrated on-the-job task performance.

RCA Radiological Controlled Area

Record Document stating results achieved or providing evidence of activities performed. A record can exist in any format. It may be physical, such as handwritten or printed documents, photographs, maps, samples, specimens and microfilm etc.

Alternatively, a record may be electronic, such as an email or database, or digitised such as a scanned image of a document or photograph.

Records Retention Schedule/Records Schedule. List detailing the type of records to be kept, their retention and review periods covering the whole lifecycle of the facility from design phase to decommissioning. The Records Schedule should provide the licensee with the means to determine the extent of its records and the means of controlling those records. The Record Retention Schedule should identify

Definitions

Reliability The probability that a component or system will perform its functions for a specified period of time when used within established operating parameters.

Residual Risk The risk has been mitigated/managed to acceptable levels.

Risk The likelihood of potential harm from a hazard being realised.

Risk An event which, if it were to occur, would have a quantifiable adverse impact on the achievement of business objectives a risk is defined as the product of the likelihood of and consequence associated with an adverse outcome

Risk Assessment A careful examination of what could cause harm so that adequate precautions are taken to prevent that harm.

Routine Work   This work is carried out on plant/equipment at a pre-determined interval of time to support: Maintenance Schedule, Mandatory/Statutory inspections, Manufacturers testing/maintenance recommendations This work is raised using model work orders that are fully pre-engineered and safety assessed.

RWP Radiological Work Permit

Radiation Work Permit (RWP) An RWP is a document that identifies all conditions and precautions for a work activity in the Radiological Controlled Area , and its requirement is created following Risk Assessment of a WO task

Safety Case All EC, safety arguments and parameters which define the safety case envelope in which the plant should be operating.

Scope Freeze Some six weeks before Execution of the Work Week, the scope of work for that week will be agreed by all Stakeholders and frozen.

Senior Authorised Person (SAP) The SAP is the person responsible for creation of Safety Documents within Safety Management track

SHIP System Health Indication Programme

Special Tools All equipment used to carry out work including equipment that requires statutory inspection, Rigging/Lifting equipment, Safety and Rescue equipment, Hydraulic lifting and pulling equipment, Portable compressed air systems, Portable pumps, Specialist or expensive equipment that requires tracking, Access equipment.

SQEP Suitably Qualified Experienced Person

SSC Systems Structures and Components – see this document for explanation

Definitions

System Aligned Work Windows (SAWW) pre-established template of work week windows within a defined cycle that aligns various systems into specific weeks. The alignment of the systems into each of the work week window templates is designed to ensure that nuclear safety, operational risk and compliance with technical specifications and licence is not challenged when work is executed in accordance with the template. These templates are used as the basis for placing work into the schedules

Three Year Rolling Plan This is a high level plan incorporating inputs from the Business Planning Rounds, Forward Engineering Plan and the Outage Management group. It will also include input from any other maintenance plans covering periods of 1 year to 5 year ahead depending upon the business requirements of the location.

Toolpouch methodology by which work is accomplished that does not require work documents to be initiated

Uniquely Tracked Commodity (UTC) A UTC is an Equipment/Component or Catalogue item which is identified in Passport by its Manufacturer Code, Model number and Serial number in order to track its installation and maintenance history. A UTC should only be attached to equipment that has a single unique Manufacturer code & Model number.

WANO World Association of Nuclear Operators

Work Management Process The process by which maintenance, modifications, surveillances, testing, engineering support, and any work activities that require plant coordination or schedule integration are implemented.

Work Order   This is the document which is used to carry out work on site which carries the full engineering specification of the work to be carried out and lists the documentation, spares, special tools and M&TE required to perform the work.

Work Request: This is the initiating electronic document within the EAM system for raising defect work.

Work Week Management The concept of Work Week Management is a process where all station resources focus on the planning and subsequent successful delivery of work packages aligned to specific Work Weeks, with minimum risk to personnel and plant safety.